BRITISH RAILWAYS
A C ELECTRIC
LOCOMOTIVES

MODERN TRACTION PROFILES

BRITISH RAILWAYS A C ELECTRIC LOCOMOTIVES

DAVID CABLE

PEN & SWORD
TRANSPORT

First published in Great Britain in 2017 by
Pen & Sword Transport
An imprint of Pen & Sword Books Ltd
47 Church Street
Barnsley
South Yorkshire
S70 2AS

ISBN 9781473896376

Printed and bound by Replika Press Pvt. Ltd.

Pen & Sword Books Ltd incorporates the imprints of Pen & Sword Archaeology, Atlas, Aviation, Battleground, Discovery, Family History, History, Maritime, Military, Naval, Politics, Railways, Select, Social History, Transport, True Crime, and Claymore Press, Frontline Books, Leo Cooper, Praetorian Press, Remember When, Seaforth Publishing and Wharncliffe.

For a complete list of Pen and Sword titles please contact:
Pen and Sword Books Limited
47 Church Street, Barnsley, South Yorkshire, S70 2AS, England
E-mail: enquiries@pen-and-sword.co.uk
Website: www.pen-and-sword.co.uk

DAVID CABLE – OTHER PUBLICATIONS

Railfreight in Colour (for the modeller and historian)
BR Passenger Sectors in Colour (for the modeller and historian)
Lost Liveries of Privatisation in Colour (for the modeller and historian)
Hydraulics in the West
The Blue Diesel Era
Rails Across North America
Rails Across Australia
Rails Across Canada
Rails Across Europe - Northern & Western
Rails Across Europe - Eastern & Southern
Rails Across Britain
Modern Traction Profiles Class 50 A Pictorial history
The Privatisation Classes

Introduction

The 1955 Modernisation of British Railways plan, amongst other things, aimed to develop a first-class system on the West Coast Main Line (WCML). In view of the deteriorating conditions for the operation and maintenance of steam locomotives, and the limited time for which they were likely to be in fit condition, modern traction was planned to take its place. In the first instance, type 4 diesel-electric locomotives were introduced – the class 40s – but their power output failed to match that of the express steam locos, thus preventing any radical changes to the existing timetables of passenger trains. Not only that, the diesel locos relied on imported fuel, the currency required for that being anathema to the Treasury in those days.

The decision was therefore taken to electrify the WCML, adopting overhead 25kv AC (OHE) as the preferred system. Experiments had been conducted with this system on the line from Lancaster to Heysham, which had been converted to this version, together with a rebuilt locomotive – the original MetroVick gas-turbine-powered loco used on the Western Region, modified for OHE operations and given class number 80.

The electrification was introduced in stages, commencing in 1960 between Crewe and Manchester Piccadilly, shortly followed by Crewe to Liverpool Lime Street. It was gradually extended to Stafford, and Stage 1 was completed with the installation through to London Euston by 1965, with the Birmingham area complex by 1967.

Stage 2 was introduced in stages, initially to Preston, and finally to Glasgow Central, where it merged into the existing Strathclyde 25kv suburban operations, the whole WCML system being fully electrified by 1974.

To operate the scheme, new traction in the form of new locomotives and multiple units had to be developed and introduced. This photo album predominantly looks at locomotives. Please note that this is not a technical book and only outline information is provided.

The AC Locomotives

Initially, contracts were issued to four private manufacturers, followed by a contract within British Railway workshops. The new locomotives were specified to meet certain criteria, such as being of Bo-Bo wheel configuration with axle loadings to meet Route Availability 6, to have a top speed of 100mph, vacuum braking, although air braking was fitted in the 1970s, and standardised semi-streamlined cabs. Each of the designs is dealt with below.

Type AL1 Class 81

Twenty-five locomotives were built by BRCW (Birmingham Railway Carriage and Wagon Company) under contract to AEI (Associated Electrical Industries). Power output was 3,380HP. They were used throughout the whole WCML, being rostered to all types of trains. As with the other members of the initial designs, they (and also the other first generation of AC locos) were nicknamed Roarers, because of the noise made by their cooling fans. The last locos were withdrawn by 1991, although some had been withdrawn earlier, one being involved in the Hixon accident. They carried BR (British Railway) electric blue and Monastral blue throughout their careers.

Type AL2 Class 82

This class was contracted by Metropolitan Vickers to be built by Beyer Peacock. Ten locomotives were built, which required some modifications, since they were originally too heavy. Power output was 3,300HP. The mercury arc rectifiers used on this class, as well as the classes 83 and 84, had a tendency to catch fire and were replaced with silicon rectifiers. They were withdrawn in 1983, after having been put into storage, although two were put back into service for a short period for empty stock duties at Euston. Apart from carrying the two shades of blue livery, one of the pilots carried Mainline colours.

Type AL3 Class 83

The fifteen locos were built by English Electric, but had a lower power output of 3,000HP. After problems with their rectifiers, they were put into storage, until refitted with silicon rectifiers, after which they worked over the whole WCML. Apart from two withdrawn after accidents, most of the class was withdrawn in the mid-1980s, although three were retained for stock working at Euston until 1989. One of these locos carried Mainline colours, all the others being in the two types of blue. This class has 'cousins' in the Polish EU/EP07 classes.

Type AL4 class 84

This class of ten 3,000HP locos, built by North British Loco Co, was probably the least successful of all the AC locos. Persistent problems caused them to be placed in storage for long periods,

and even after being fitted with silicon rectifiers, they were still not that reliable. Withdrawal was complete by 1980, although one loco was converted as a load bank tester. The pioneer loco has been preserved at the NRM (National Railway Museum). In standard condition they carried the two blue colours. The load bank testing loco was painted blue and red.

Type AL5 class 85

This was probably the most successful of the first generation of AC locomotives. Built at the BR workshops at Doncaster, the forty locos, were subsequently sub-divided into twenty-five 100mph units and fifteen re-geared for freight duties, with a maximum speed of 80mph. They had a power output of 3.200HP. Originally fitted with germanium rectifiers, they were all modified with the silicon type. They were withdrawn in 1991, having carried only the two blue colour schemes.

No names were applied to any of these five locomotives designs. Examples of all these five AL classes have been preserved.

Type AL6 Class 86

This type of AC locomotive became the standard class from the 1960s, and numbered 100 units. They were built at both the BR workshops at Doncaster and English Electric at Vulcan Foundry. They were basically 100mph engines, although variations shown below were introduced. Power output ranged from 3,600 to 4,040 to 5,000HP depending on the sub-classes, which are listed below. They were developed from the previous classes, with a flat, rather than rounded, cab front, and the cooling fan arrangements reduced the noise emitted by the first five classes. The major problem that they caused was that they had axle hung motors, instead of frame mounted, which caused substantial damage to the track, necessitating redesigning of the suspension. The class 86 was a very much all-purpose loco, used on high-speed passenger duties, mail and parcel trains, and a variety of freight traffic. Their duties were undertaken on the West Coast lines and the East Anglian lines to Norwich, Harwich and Cambridge. A few mail services were worked on the ECML (East Coast Main Line).

The sub-classes of the class 86 were:

86/0 The locomotives which retained their original suspension. After most had been modified to another sub-section, they became limited to 80mph. In this form, they were mainly restricted to freight working.

86/1 A version of the 86/2, fettled for 110mph maximum speed.

86/2 This sub-class contained the engines which were modified from the original class 86/0 by the addition of external flexicoil springs and new wheels. They retained 100mph speed and operated express passenger services.

86/3 Some 86/0s had new wheels, allowing them to return to 100mph working.

86/4 All remaining class 86/0 and 86/3 locos were fitted with the new suspension to make them equivalent to 86/2.

86/5 This comprised a single loco which had its power output raised so as to be at a level similar to that of the class 90.

86/6 Ex-86/4 engines with electric train heating removed, and a 75mph limit applied, to make them suitable for freight work.

86/9 Two locos converted for mobile load bank testing.

Operators

Following privatisation, the class 86 locomotives used by British Rail were taken over by Virgin – West Coast and Cross Country – Anglia, EWS and Freightliner. One loco was used by Hull Trains for a limited period. Apart from preserved units, a few have been sold to European organisations in Hungary and Bulgaria.

Colour Schemes
    BR Monastral Blue
    Inter City/Mainline
    L & M 150 (86214,86235}
    Parcels/RES
    Network SouthEast (86401)
    Railfreight Distribution
    Railfreight General (86502,86627)
    Freightliner Grey/Green/Powerhaul
    Virgin Red
    Virgin Caledonian Blue (86245)
    Anglia
    EWS
    Colas Railfreight (86701)
    Miscellaneous (e.g. Europhoenix, Rail Traction)

Names
    The class 86s have carried a wide selection of names, ranging from Cities, Regiments, Institutions, and notable persons to old locos of the LNWR (London and North Western Railway).

Class 87

With the extension of the WCML electrification to Scotland, additional locomotives were required, leading to the introduction of the class 87 in the early 1970s. Thirty-six locos were built with 110mph maximum speed and 5,000HP power output. One loco was classified as 87/1, being fitted with thyristor power control. This class worked exclusively on the WCML, and were the flagship locos on this line until the early part of the twenty-first century, when they were usurped by Pendolino EMUs. More than half the class has been exported to Bulgaria following withdrawal of the class. One is still in service with Caledonian Sleeper and is used on charter services.

Operators
    British Rail
    Virgin West Coast
    Cotswold Rail
    DRS
    First Group
    Caledonian Sleeper

Colour Schemes
    BR Monastral Blue
    Inter City
    Large Logo Charcoal (87006)
    Railfreight Distribution (87101)
    Virgin Red
    Porterbrook (87002)
    DRS/First Group (87006/22/28)
    Cotswold Rail (87007/8)
    Acorp LNWR (87019)
    Network SouthEast (87012)

Names
    The class 87 names were mainly of historical figures and cities. Nameplates were of standard BR design, with the exception of that on 87101 which was in stainless steel.

Class 88

At the time of writing this book, the class 88 has yet to appear in the UK, although it has been under test in the Czech Republic. The locos have a Bo-Bo configuration, and are electro-diesels fitted with a small Caterpillar engine. They will have 100mph capability. The class 88 is being built by Vossloh in Spain.

Class 89

The unique class 89 was built by Brush in 1986, to a BR outline specification for a locomotive to become the standard for the forthcoming East Coast Main Line (ECML). A Co-Co wheel arrangement was used, the only one of the AC electric loco classes (excepting the class 80). Almost 6,000HP provided, with a top speed capability of 125mph (although this was never applied in everyday service). Being a one-off without a spare parts back-up, it spent considerable time sidelined from occasional failures and was initially withdrawn in 1992. However, it was returned to service following privatisation until 2001, and has now been preserved.

    After initial trials on the WCML, it was transferred to the ECML, where it was regularly seen on services between London and the West Riding of Yorkshire.

Operators
    British Rail
    GNER

Colour Schemes
    Inter City
    GNER with Gold Letters/Silver Letters

Name
    The locomotive was named *Avocet* in 1989.

Class 90

Originally classified before entry into service as class 87/2, the class 90 is a Bo-Bo locomotive of 5,000HP built by BREL at Crewe from 1987. Fifty locomotives were built, primarily to replace the earlier classes 81-85, several of which had become increasingly unreliable. They incorporated new technology, and from the outset were fitted for push-pull operation with driving trailers at the other end of a train.

In the early 1990s, half the fleet was modified for freight operation, reclassified 90/1, and their previous maximum speed of 110mph was reduced to 75mph.

The class 90 was used by several operators, and was bestowed with a wide selection of liveries, as are shown below.

Operators
> British Rail
> Freightliner
> Virgin
> EWS/DB Schenker
> One/National Express/Abellio Greater Anglia
> First Group

Colours
> InterCity/Mainline
> Railfreight Distribution
> Freightliner Grey/Green/Powerhaul
> RES
> Virgin Red
> EWS
> DB Schenker
> First ScotRail (90019/21/4)
> One
> One with dark grey body (90003/4)
> National Express
> Abellio Greater Anglia
> Malcolm (90024)
> DRS (90034)
> GNER (unbranded) (90024)
> Deutsche Bahn (90129)
> SNCB (90128)
> SNCF (90130)

Names
> Several of the class 90s have been named. Those working

on the services from Liverpool Street to Norwich carry names with East Anglian connections, the Freightliner locos relate to their terminals, the three locos in European colours were named Freight Connection in their own languages, as well as 90022 in English. Others were of a miscellaneous nature.

Class 91
This class was introduced to operate services in conjunction with the electrification of the East Coast Main Line in the late 1980s. They were built for a maximum speed of 140mph, working with tilting passenger stock, although in practice this was not used, the locos working to a maximum of 125mph. The thirty-one locos are of Bo-Bo configuration, and have a power output of just on 6,500HP. The locos were designed to be able to work freight services, and had a second cab fitted to a blunt end (with 110mph limit), although this type of work was never used with the class. However when equipment failed within the streamlined front cab, passenger trains were run with the loco blunt end first.

The class was refurbished during the early 2000s, the locos being reclassified 91/1.

When first introduced, the locos were maintained at BREL (British Rail Engineering Limited), Crewe, allowing them to be seen on the WCML running light engine, but with the exception of a special series of trials between Euston and Glasgow, have always been seen only on the ECML.

Operators
> British Rail
> GNER
> National Express
> East Coast
> Virgin Trains East Coast

Colours InterCity
> GNER with Gold/Silver letters
> National Express
> East Coast Silver
> Virgin East Coast
> Flying Scotsman purple (91101)
> Flying Scotsman VEC with Saltires (91101)
> *Battle of Britain Flight* (91110)
> *For the Fallen* (91111)
> Miscellaneous short term (e.g. *Skyfall, Christmas*)

Names
> The class has carried a wide variety of names, ranging from *HM The Queen* through to locations, organisations and people.

Class 92

The class 92 was developed for Channel Tunnel services in the mid-1990s. The locomotives are dual-voltage machines, operating off both 25kv overhead AC systems and 750v third rail pick-up.

They were conceived as mixed-traffic locomotives, intended for operating freight trains generally from southern England to France, and also overnight passenger services from the English Midlands also to France. In the event, the latter never eventuated, although in recent times, the class has undertaken passenger duties with the Caledonian Sleeper services.

The locos are of a Co-Co configuration. Power output varies from 6,750HP with AC OHE to 5,350HP from third rail. The class contains forty-five engines, and was built by Brush and ABB. The maximum speed is 87mph.

The failure to meet forecasts of rail-based freight through the tunnel, and the failure to commence the passenger services, has resulted in the class being seriously underutilised, to the extent that not only have a number of locos been stored, but nine have been sold to Romania and Bulgaria. Consequently, seeing class 92s working under AC wiring has been very limited.

Operators
> British Rail
> SNCF
> EWS/DB Schenker
> GBRF/Europorte

Colours Two-tone grey with roundels
> Railfreight Distribution (92022/30)
> EWS (92001/31)
> DB Schenker
> GB Railfreight/Europorte
> Stobart Rail (92017)

Names
> The class is named after British and European composers and writers.

Summary

The AC electric locomotives transformed operations on three major routes from the 1960s up to today. Although suffering technical problems in their early days, and being unable to perform when overhead infrastructure fails, they have fulfilled their early promise, and contributed to running world-class conventional services.

This album uses photographs, which unless otherwise mentioned, are all of my own taking. Some early shots using dubious quality film, which has deteriorated over the years, have been, I hope, rectified to a reasonable extent using Photoshop. Several of the photos have been taken at the same locations. I make no excuses for this – these spots remain free from foliage and platform edges, and are within reasonable distance of a day out from Hampshire.

In particular, the photos taken on the southern section of the WCML have brought back happy memories of steam train spotting at these locations in the late 1940s. Happy days, then and, until recently, now!

> *David Cable*
> *Hartley Wintney, Hants, UK*
> *September 2016*

Class 80
The former gas turbine-powered engine, converted as a test bed for operation with 25KV overhead electrification, stands on Wath Shed after withdrawal. (DC Collection)

Class 81 Type AL1
Class 81 81018 is seen north of Berkhamstead in June 1975, with an unidentified Up express working. What the white embellishments between the first two vents are, I have no idea.

81002 is standing at Nuneaton in June 1976, waiting for its next turn of duty some time in the future.

A panned shot of 81007 seen working a Down express in August 1978. The view is taken at Horton, just north of Cheddington, a location now totally ruined by foliage.

81021 exits Tring Cutting and passes the cement works at Pitstone with a northbound Freightliner service in August 1978. Note at least one container in the original Freightliner colours.

81011 stands ready at Platform 1 at Euston to take the empty stock of an express back to the sidings at Stonebridge Park for cleaning. A class 08 keeps it company in October 1983.

The autumn mists are still hanging around at Ledburn Junction in October 1984, where 81020 passes with a northbound train of stone hoppers.

Identified as a class 81 by the white salmon emblem, but without being able to catch the number, a southbound freight train is seen just south of Carnforth in February 1985. Note the wide variety of rolling stock in this service.

81009 exits the yards at Mossend with a train of limestone empties in February 1989. Waiting for work in the yards are a class 08, a class 47 and a class 87.

Beautifully restored to its original Electric Blue colour scheme and number, class 81 E3003 is seen on display at the open day at Worksop in September 1993.

Class 82 Type AL2
Class 82 82004 stands in Manchester Piccadilly Station in June 1974, waiting for the right-away signal to depart with its train for Plymouth.

Class 82 82002 is about to enter Stowe Hill Tunnel with a Down express in September 1978. (Gavin Morrison)

Passing Charnock Richard, north of Wigan, in August 1981, 82008 is working a Crewe to Preston semi-fast service. (Gavin Morrison)

Class 82 82001 and class 81 81020 are seen stabled alongside Crewe South Shed in August 1981.

82008, seen in standard BR Monastral Blue, was on display at the open day at Crewe Basford Hall in August 1995.

Class 83 Type AL3

Class 83 83009 and an unidentified class 81 pass Headstone Lane in May 1976 with a Halewood to Dagenham Ford container service, making a change from the Cup Final specials that day.

A panned close-up of 83006 working a Down freight service past Horton, near Cheddington, in August 1978. This view shows what a neat design was this class of electric locomotive.

Passing Tamworth Low Level at speed, 83007 is working an Up express in August 1980. (Gavin Morrison)

Also seen at the open day at Crewe Basford Hall in August 1995 was 83012, surrounded by much detritus. As one of the engines used for empty stock workings at Euston at one time, it was repainted into Mainline colours – InterCity without any branding.

Class 84 Type AL4
Stored at Longsight in 1961, class 84 E3045 is stored with another in May 1961, no doubt having had some of the problems affecting this class. (Gavin Morrison)

With a nice selection of freight wagons in tow, a very smart-looking class 84 84002 is seen on the Up relief line at Floriston in September 1979. Note the height of the catenary at this crossing.

84003 stands in Birmingham New Street Station, as it was in August 1980. (Gavin Morrison)

One class 84 was converted as a Mobile Load Bank. The loco was originally 84009, renumbered as ADB 968021, and repainted into departmental red and blue with wrap-round yellow side cab window surrounds. It was photographed in the stabling sidings at Cricklewood in May 1982.

Class 85 Type AL5
Class 85 85010 and class 86 86021 will shortly pass through Hatch End Station with an Up express in May 1976. This is another photo taken at what is now a location covered in foliage.

Class 85 85038 enters Stafford Station with a southbound inter-regional express in July 1979.

85012 heads a trainload of pallet vans, working its way northwards through Lichfield Trent Valley in July 1979.

With the disused water tower in the background, a train of BOC tanks heads north through Tamworth Low Level behind 85012 in July 1979.

An unidentified class 85 works south at Ledburn Junction, with what I think was a Stirling to Kensington Olympia motorail service. The date was August 1980.

Whilst rushing to catch a train in March 1982, I could not resist this shot of a class 85 standing at Nuneaton at the head of an MGR coal train. Time did not allow for me to get the number.

With sixteen coaches in tow, 85025 speeds along the down main line at Betley Road in July 1982. What the working was I have no idea, although it was probably an empty stock duty.

Class 85 85024 is in the process of backing down onto its coaches, prior to departure from Euston in October 1983.

On the Up slow line at Ledburn Junction, 85039 heads a lightly-loaded Freightliner service in October 1984.

Following the previous train, a fully-loaded Freightliner works south behind another class 85.

More action at Ledburn Junction in October 1984, this time showing class 85 85034 working a train of BOC tanks from North Wembley to Widnes.

A murky day in April 1985 sees a class 85 heading north through Acton Bridge with an unidentified passenger service.

Once upon a time, fans hired a series of special trains to attend football Cup Finals at Wembley. One such working, a first-class premium special, passes the site of Bushey water troughs behind a class 85 in April 1985. Manchester United beat Everton 1-0, so presumably someone was happy.

A class 85 ambles along the Down slow line just north of Hatch End in May 1985, with a Down Freightliner.

Class 85 85004 leads 87101 *Stephenson* and a test coach running south of Winwick Junction in April 1985.

Greenholme Bridge is now encumbered with railings, but in April 1985, one could lean over the bridge wall without any problem. This enabled me to take a class 85 descending the bank from Shap Summit with an Up express.

Pulling off the A74, a view of the line on the south side of Beattock Summit could be obtained, where another class 85 was heading north with an express in April 1985.

The following year, another Cup Final train – not a premium one this time – passes Harrow & Wealdstone on the Up slow line. The class 85 does the honours in May 1986.

Class 85 85014 zooms through Bletchley Station in March 1987, with a Down Freightliner service. The out-of-use flyover may yet be brought back into action, one hopes!

Creeping through Crewe Station in December 1987, 85020 has two coaches in tow, one in Trans Pennine/Regional Rail colours, the other in InterCity. A strange working, but worthy of a photo.

Looking like a model train, a class 85 works north near Madeley in June 1989 with an interesting selection of freight vehicles.

With a backdrop of containers, class 85 85038 passes the time of day at Ripple Lane in October 1989. It will have something to do sometime!

One of the class 85s re-geared for freight duties, 85109, passes Watford Junction in February 1990 with a northbound Freightliner service. Network SouthEast signs and red paint make themselves noticed.

Class 86 Type AL6

Timing had to be spot on for this shot of class 86 86204 exiting the tunnel at Linslade, north of Leighton Buzzard, in May 1974. It was working a Euston to Birmingham express.

Although the train is slightly blurred, the location is of too much interest to omit. The location is north of Roade, and the structures in the foreground carry the catenary and support the walls of the Northampton lines, which drop away from the main line. The class 86 was working a Glasgow-bound express. Taken in September 1974.

86211 hauls a short train of vans north of Berkhamstead and heading north in June 1975. Note the amount of catenary support, and compare it with what has been erected over the Great Western line in the Thames Valley!

Seen from the Up platform at Nuneaton, 86237 rushes past the station with a Down Manchester service in June 1976.

The rain has stopped, and the passengers wait to get into their Wolverhampton to Euston express, which has stopped at Coventry in June 1976. Class 86 86214 heads the train on this dull summer day.

The loco-hauled Up Manchester Pullman approaches Nuneaton in June 1976, hauled by 86224.

An interesting contrast between the modern electric locomotive and its train of old wagons. 86006 was seen in August 1978 south of Berkhamstead. The original scissors-type pantograph shows up clearly.

Class 86 86206 zooms above me near Berkhamstead with a Euston to Glasgow express in August 1978.

Class 86 86233, which looks ex-works, arrives at Stafford with an inter-regional express from Bristol to Liverpool in July 1979.

86235 negotiates the junction at Colwich, which it passes on its way from Euston to Manchester Piccadilly in July 1979.

Names have now started to be applied to the AC electric locos. 86241 *Glenfiddich* rounds the reverse curves at Rugeley with a Euston to Manchester express in June 1979. Rugeley Power Station looms in the background.

86225 passes Lichfield Trent Valley in June 1979, working from Euston to Carlisle with a semi-fast service.

A panned shot of class 86 86214 *Sans Pareil* gives the full effect of the livery carried by this loco and 86235 *Novelty,* celebrating the 150th anniversary of the opening of the Liverpool and Manchester Railway in 1830. The Large Logo scheme is enhanced by a yellow band carrying the crests of the associated communities, plus the BR logo. The names of the two locos were those of two of the entrants in the trials. The photo was taken at Ledburn Junction in August 1980.

The other L & M loco, 86235 *Novelty*, is seen entering Crewe Station with a Euston to Holyhead express in August 1981. The class 86 will be replaced by a class 47 at this point.

A most unexpected and interesting working was seen at Crewe in August 1981. 86230 *The Duke of Wellington* arrived from the north with a test train heading for Derby, comprising various test coaches and a selection of frames with the outline of the future APT coaches. Note the variations in the degree of tilt.

In the days when mail and parcels traffic was a staple commodity for railway haulage, parcels are unloaded from the front van of a train, which has arrived at Euston one evening in December 1982, behind 86256 *Pebble Mill.*

The Manchester Pullman was one of the first trains to carry the new InterCity livery. It is seen here having arrived at Euston in October 1983, behind 86226 *Mail*, a name originally carried by an LNWR locomotive.

At the other end of the train, 86311 *Airey Neave* has now coupled on to take the empty stock to the carriage sheds at Stonebridge Park. An unrecorded class 87 stands in the adjacent platform.

86305 speeds past through Bushey and Oxhey Station with a southbound parcels service in April 1985.

86258 *Talyllyn* approaches Bushey and Oxhey with an express from Euston to Liverpool in April 1985.

Running over the site of where the water troughs used to be at Bushey, an unidentified class 86 is seen in April 1985 hauling an express bound for Birmingham.

The view from Little Oxhey Lane Bridge, between Hatch End and Carpenders Park, includes class 86s on Up and Down expresses about to pass each other in April 1985. No details could be obtained.

The view at Greenholme in April 1985 is free from trees and railings, enabling a clear shot to be taken of 86312 *Elizabeth Garret Anderson* climbing up to Shap summit with a Birmingham to Glasgow express.

Now in newly-applied InterCity livery, 86238 arrives at Euston in September 1985 with an express from Wolverhampton, comprising a mix of liveries.

The Stockport to Stalybridge Bubble Car disappears into the distance, as 86258 *Talyllyn* approaches through the tunnel of steelwork over the viaduct at Stockport, with an inter-regional express from Manchester Piccadilly in April 1986.

An InterCity-liveried class 86 speeds up the main-line tracks at Harrow and Wealdstone in May 1986, with an express from Birmingham to Euston.

A Liverpool Street to Norwich express approaches Manningtree station in May 1986, the train being hauled by 86255 *Penrith Beacon*.

Working in the opposite direction, 86217 *City University* clatters over the junction for the Harwich branch in May 1986, with a Liverpool Street-bound express from Norwich.

86205 *City of Lancaster* is ready to carry on from its stop at Ipswich with a Norwich to Liverpool Street express in May 1986.

A Manchester to Euston express hurtles through another tunnel of steelwork, this time at Bletchley, in March 1987, behind class 86 86408.

Rugby Station, as it used to be in all its glory, where 86410 has arrived for a short stop whilst working from Carlisle to Euston in March 1987.

A train of steel coils from Ravenscraig to Shotton climbs up to Shap Summit in March 1987, behind 86422 and 86421 *London School of Economics*. Note that the coils are eye to the sun, which can cause damage to the whole coil if badly handled.

Having driven down the M6 – at legal speeds of course - I managed to get another shot of this train passing Winwick Junction.

Looking the other way at Winwick, 86414 *Frank Hornby*, with an unidentified class 81, heads north, returning the empty steel coil wagons to Ravenscraig in March 1987.

Norwich Station in June 1987 hosts 86233 *Laurence Olivier* arriving with an express from Norwich, whilst on the right Norwich's pet station pilot, 08869 *The Canary*, waits for business. Note the Stratford-style silver roof on the class 86.

Another express from Liverpool Street arrives at Norwich in June 1987, this one being hauled by 86256 *Pebble Mill*. A mail van is the penultimate vehicle in the train formation.

InterCity colours have replaced the L & M 150 scheme on 86214 *Sans Pareil,* which has arrived at Cambridge with a service from Liverpool Street in July 1987. All the people on the platform must be meeting passengers, since this train terminated here.

To celebrate twenty one years of the Inter City brand, BR decided to repaint 86426 in a semblance of the original electric blue colours, but the shade of blue was nowhere near the original scheme. The engine is seen in February 1988, after arrival at Liverpool Lime Street with an express from Euston. It also carried its original number, E3195, and metal lion and wheel crest.

Class 86 86225 *Hardwicke* thunders through Kings Langley in May 1988, with an express from Manchester Piccadilly to Euston.

Glasgow Central is the location for this shot of 86223 *Norwich Union* leaving the station with a train of mail and parcel vans, gleaming on a dull day in May 1988.

With 86251 *The Birmingham Post* second from the right, and 81007 on the right, Willesden S hed also hosts representatives of classes 87 and 90 in January 1989.

Exiting the avoiding lines tunnel at Crewe, 86438 and 86439 climb the incline with a train of steel coils from Ravenscraig to South Wales. It is February 1989, and the works has now learnt the right way to load the coils!

Only one class 86 was painted in Network SouthEast colours, to celebrate electric traction being able to work to Cambridge. Now in more familiar territory, 86401 has stopped at Watford Junction in February 1989 with an unidentified Euston-bound express.

The Freightliner terminal at Gartsherrie (Coatbridge) is preparing an intermodal service for Felixstowe in February 1989. 86502 *Lloyds List* heads the train. This loco was only one of four on British Rail which carried the Railfreight General decals, although they were not carried at this juncture.

With its pantograph fully stretched, 86418 passes Watery Lane in the West Midlands, with one of the longer-distance inter-regional services, namely Glasgow Central to Penzance, seen in June 1989.

86245 *Dudley Castle* is fairly near its namesake, as it is seen near Coseley with a Liverpool to Plymouth express in June 1989. Note that the restaurant car is at the back, not making life easy for passengers in the front of the train!

Another train of steel coils from Ravenscraig has paused for breath at Warrington Bank Quay in November 1989, with class 86 86609 leading class 87 87013 *John o' Gaunt* doing the honours up front.

An against-the-light shot at Crewe in February 1990 could not be avoided if I was to record 86627 *The Industrial Society* carrying the Railfreight General decals. This loco, 86502 and 50149, carried these in daily service, and a class 60, 60010, was so adorned purely for the 1991 Railfreight Distribution calendar.

With proper InterCity branding, 86405 heads towards Euston in February 1990, as does the class 313 on the DC lines, but the analogy of the Tortoise and the Hare won't apply in this case!

With a little glint highlighting the consist, 86234 *J. B. Priestley O.M.* heads a northbound empty mail and parcels train with an interesting mix of coaching stock..

A pair of class 86s with Railfreight Distribution decals, 86636 and 86603, arrive at Crewe in January 1991, with a selection of vans, and, most interestingly, behind the engines, ex-class 25 train heating unit *Ethel 3* in Mainline colours.

Mailbags are loaded and unloaded one night at Crewe in January 1991, where 86259 *Peter Pan* has brought a Euston to Manchester express into platform 6.

In March 1991, a Norwich to Liverpool Street express, in complete Inter City colours, passes Bethnal Green behind 86238 *European Community*, and starts the steep descent to its destination.

Preston Station is the setting for this shot of 86216 *Meteor*, which has stopped on its way with an express from Inverness to Euston in July 1991. Like the old station at Rugby, this is another station with LNWR character.

The plain parcels livery was quite quickly replaced by the Rail Express version (RES), so shots of class 86s in the original colour were not that common. So, to illustrate the design, 86424 is seen passing Ledburn Junction in March 1992, with a short Up parcels service, with a variety of vans and colours.

Another train has just cleared the way for me to be able to take 86639 and 86627 *The Industrial Society*, both with RFD decals, passing Homerton in July 1993. They were hauling a Crewe Basford Hall to Felixstowe Freightliner.

Seven months later, and one stop further east, a similar service is being worked by 86636 and 86633 *Wulfruna*, which are seen at Hackney Wick in February 1994.

A Parcels Sector-liveried loco, 86241 *Glenfiddich*, hauls a matched set of RES vans past Winwick in February 1994.

An Up parcels service sweeps round the sharp curve at Wolverton in May 1995, headed by a pair of RES-liveried class 86s, 86426 being the lead loco.

Another mail and parcels service, this time from Crewe to Euston, comprises a mixture of vans hauled by Res 86430 *Saint Edmund* and 86261. They are seen at Headstone Lane in July 1996.

In a distinct version of the standard Virgin colours, 86245 *Caledonian* was repainted in a Scottish blue scheme, but without the company's name. It is seen passing Carpenders Park in May 1998, with a Euston to Birmingham express.

Now in Freightliner green, 86636 and 86609 pass Headstone Lane with a Lawley Street to Felixstowe intermodal service in July 1999.

Class 86s in full red Virgin colours were quite rare on the Great Eastern section, normally having received a more appropriate colour scheme. However, 86209 *City of Coventry* was seen in August 2002 passing Pudding Mill Lane on its way from Liverpool Street to Norwich.

A Birmingham to Euston express passes South Kenton in September 2002, being worked by 86261 *The Rail Charter Partnership,* which carries EWS colours.

Specially decorated in blue, 86233 *Alstom Heritage*, which also carried number E3172, passes Headstone Lane in January 2003 with a Euston to Birmingham express.

A pair of Freightliner class 86s – 86426 and 86631 – creep through Ipswich Station on their way from Trafford Park to the holding sidings at Ipswich in June 2003.

With a Union flag surmounted on the standard Anglia colour scheme to commemorate the celebration, the appropriately-named 86227 *Golden Jubilee* accelerates away from Colchester in November 2003, with a Liverpool Street to Norwich express.

A diverted Liverpool Street to Norwich express works north through Harlow Town in July 2004, being propelled by Anglia 86230. Note the number on the front end.

The two class 86s used for mobile load bank testing are seen stabled at Rugby in June 2005. In the yellow Network Rail colours, 86901 *Chief Engineer* partners 86902 *Rail Vehicle Engineering*.

The Freightliner class 86, 86501, which was boosted to have a power output similar to that of the class 90s, gets going from its crew change at Willesden, and is seen near Kenton with a Felixstowe to Trafford Park intermodal service in July 2007.

Framed by the catenary supports at Atherstone, 86639 and 86605 are seen close-up, heading north with a Freightliner from Tilbury to Crewe in April 2011.

Class 87
Class 87 87008 waits for the signal to start away from Euston in November 1973, with an express bound for Liverpool.

With brake dust staining the body side, 87003 heads south near Berkhamstead in June 1975, with a Liverpool to Euston express.

At the south end of Nuneaton Station in June 1976, 87025 runs through non-stop with an express from Euston to Glasgow.

Still fitted with the original pantograph, 87027 *Wolf of Badenoch* looks impressive as it speeds towards London, seen near Berkhamstead working a Liverpool to Euston express.

This Glasgow to Euston express clatters over the layout at Colwich Junction behind 87005 *City of Liverpool* in July 1979.

The signal box stands proud in the middle of Lichfield Trent Valley Station, from behind which 87010 *King Arthur* emerges with a train from Holyhead to Euston in July 1979.

Another rather dirty class 87 sweeps past Ledburn Junction in August 1980. The locomotive is 87034 *William Shakespeare*, which is working an express from Euston to Glasgow.

87024 *Lord of the Isles* is seen one night in December 1982, having arrived at Euston with an unidentified express.

Timing had to be spot on to frame 87101 *Stephenson* emerging from Stowe Hill Tunnel in May 1983. The working was not recorded. Note the stainless steel nameplate carried by this locomotive.

87002 *Royal Sovereign* comes down the bank from Camden and enters platform 1 at Euston Station with a train from Birmingham New Street in October 1983.

The introduction of the InterCity brand in 1984 gave rise to a new livery. However, an experimental livery was carried for a short period by 87006 *City of Glasgow*. Seen at the Crewe Works open day in June 1984, the engine is seen in the unique Charcoal Grey Large Logo scheme, unfortunately not cleaned as well as it might have been.

On a rather misty day in October 1984, a visit to Ledburn Junction provided three successive shots of class 87s. First was 87005 *City of London* working a Down Freightliner service.

Next, working a Manchester Piccadilly to Euston express, was 87012 *Coeur de Lion,* which carried the prototype InterCity livery with black BR logos on the cab sides.

Third and last was Charcoal Grey 87006 *City of Glasgow* heading towards its namesake destination. As a matter of interest these three trains had been preceded by the APT in full flow, working from Glasgow to Euston and making for a worthwhile day.

87018 *Lord Nelson* approaches Hatch End Station with a Down express for Manchester Piccadilly in April 1985. In the distance the Kodak Works is silhouetted.

Looking very smart in freshly applied InterCity colours, 87008 *City of Liverpool* nears Hatch End with an express from its namesake city in May 1985. One IC coach mars the train consist.

In the prototype InterCity colours, 87018 *Lord Nelson* stops at Oxenholme in April 1985, with an express from Glasgow Central to Euston.

A quite dirty 87011 *The Black Prince* passes Oxenholme non-stop on its way to Glasgow Central from Birmingham in April 1985.

Class 87 87017 *Iron Duke* is seen near Lambrigg in April 1985, with a Glasgow Central to Euston express. Pity the sun wasn't out!

A scene at Crewe with plenty of human activity, as 87010 *King Arthur* arrives with an express from Euston, destined for Carlisle in October 1985. It is 1108, and the train is only two minutes late!

Still carrying BR blue colours, 87030 *Black Douglas* speeds past Farington Junction, on its way from Euston to Glasgow in February 1986, but will shortly apply the brakes for its stop at Preston.

A filthy 87003 *Patriot* passes Bescot with an empty stock train in April 1986. In those days the holding sidings often contained something of interest; on this occasion there were examples of classes 20, 58 and 86 (and, out of sight, 25, 47, 56 and 85).

InterCity 87012 in May 1986, at that time between names, rushes through Hatch End in the days before a fence precluded taking photos of the main-line tracks from this platform. The train was not identified.

It is 11:50 and all is well at Rugby in March 1987, where 87009 *City of Birmingham* has drawn to a halt with an express bound for Holyhead. What a lovely old station it used to be.

In a picturesque setting at the end of the Lune Gorge near Low Gill, 87003 *Patriot* heads south from Glasgow Central to Euston in February 1988.

Super power is rostered for an empty stock working, leaving Glasgow Central in March 1988, behind 87006 *Glasgow Garden Festival* and 87034 *William Shakespeare*, both locos under power.

87028 *Lord President* ambles through Crewe Station with a Euston to Liverpool express, whilst 47606 *Odin* has just backed on to the Holyhead-bound express in platform 5. Taken in February 1989.

87025 *County of Cheshire* (it should be *County of Chester* – Cheshire is the county name) has arrived at Wolverhampton in September 1989 with a Brighton to Manchester service, which it has taken over in Birmingham New Street.

A February 1990 shower has enhanced the lighting at Crewe, where 87008 *City of Liverpool* arrives with an express bound for Liverpool Lime Street.

The glory of the Lune Gorge near Tebay adds to the view of 87015 *Howard of Effingham* propelling its Glasgow to Euston express in June 1991. Driving trailers are now in vogue. Note how uncluttered the M6 Motorway is.

A Euston to Glasgow Central express is about to enter and stop at Preston in July 1991. At the head of the train is 87030 *Black Douglas*.

Closure of the West Coast Main Line at Stonebridge Park, due to work on the North Circular Road, results in Liverpool services being diverted to the Midland main line. At Sharnbrook in October 1991, 87021 *Robert the Bruce* is towed dead behind a down service.

Under its own power, **87024** *Lord of the Isles* speeds north through Harlington with a down St Pancras to Liverpool express. Definitely not your everyday sighting on this line, and no other enthusiasts were present! Taken in October 1991.

Something of a comedown for 87101 *Stephenson,* which has lost its express status, and has now been transferred to Railfreight. In Railfreight Grey with Distribution Sector decals, it was photographed at the open day at Worksop in September 1993.

In full Virgin colours, a Euston to Glasgow express negotiates the reverse curves at Slindon in June 2000, with 87021 *Robert the Bruce* providing the power.

Quite what a driving trailer was doing between 87029 *Earl Marischal* and its train, I have no idea. A Wolverhampton to Euston express was passing South Kenton in September 2003 for this photo.

ROSCO Porterbrook had five of its locomotives decorated in its house colours, one of them being 87002, which had a different scheme on each side. This view shows the loco running light engine past Headstone Lane on a Willesden to Watford Junction test run in September 2003.

The other side of Porterbrook's 87002 is seen in this view of a Euston to Birmingham service, unusually on the slow line, passing South Kenton in March 2005.

A handful of class 87s appeared in various colour schemes towards the end of their careers. One such was 87019 *ACoRP: Association of Community Rail Partnerships,* which was given an almost LNWR colour scheme. It is seen working a Wolverhampton – Euston express at Headstone Lane in March 2005.

Another one-off was 87012, decorated in NSE colours, named *The Olympian,* and with a promotion message for the 2012 London Olympic Bid. Passing Headstone Lane in August 2005, it is hauling a train which started at Victoria behind 66715 *Valour,* and travelled to Bescot via Reading, and then Crewe, where 87012 took over for the return to Euston.

87019 *ACoRP* is seen again, this time in April 2006 at Carpenders Park with the Wembley Railnet to Shieldmuir set of three class 325 mail units.

DRS acquired three class 87s for a short period, before they were taken on by First Group. Although without any branding, DRS 87006 passes Rugby non-stop with an express from Birmingham International to Euston in June 2006.

The Olympian, **87012**, is now seen hauling the Wembley Railnet to Shieldmuir class 325s near Kenton in June 2006, complete with headboard reading *Vulture Squadron*, Saltires on the buffers, and a small St George's flag above the central headlight.

The amazing sight at Cholsey of three class 87s being hauled from Wembley to Long Marston in January 2008, by 66726. At the rear is First Group ex-DRS 87028, next is 87002 in faded Porterbrook purple, and next to the class 66 is ex-DRS 87022. Not on the usual Western Region menu!

Several class 87s have been sold to Bulgaria, three of them being seen leaving Long Marston after preparation. Former Cotswold Rail locos 87008 and 87007 retain their white livery, but now have new emblems, and 87026 is in a Bulgarian livery. The train is hauled by 66723 and is travelling to Crewe in April 2008.

Class 88

Class 88 88002 is seen on test at the Velim test track in the Czech Republic in 2016, hauling a trainload of coal hoppers. Looking very similar to the class 68, it has yet to acquire any signs of ownership by DRS. (Quintus Vosman)

Class 89

The unique class 89, 89001, starts away from Crewe Works with a test train to Stafford in July 1987, with 85031 rostered inside in case of trouble.

89001 gleams as a result of the efforts of Bounds Green Shed to provide a train worthy of working the *Mallard* Fiftieth Anniversary special from Kings Cross to Doncaster in July 1998. The train is seen at Hatfield running at full line speed.

89001 carried different versions of InterCity colours during its lifetime, and was later named *Avocet*. It is seen here posed at Bounds Green Shed in November 1988.

Subsequent to withdrawal from BR due to spare parts problems, it was returned to service, following privatisation, by GNER. It is seen at Brookmans Park in March 1997, working from Leeds to Kings Cross. Note that it carries the short-term silver company letters instead of the usual gold.

Class 90

At the open day at Crewe Works in July 1987, a locomotive was under construction. It carries the chalked-on number 87201, since the build was to be an extension of the class 87. In the event, it went into service as the first class 90, number 90001.

90005 *Financial Times* passes through Watford Junction in April 1988, with a northbound driver training special working. These locos never appeared in BR Blue.

At Watery Lane, between Tipton and Dudley Port in the West Midlands, 90019 propels a Wolverhampton to Euston express past the loops in June 1989.

A Birmingham International to Manchester Piccadilly service is seen near Coseley in August 1989. 90021 heads the train, in which the restaurant car is placed relatively inconveniently at the front of the train.

A Liverpool Lime Street to Poole inter-regional passes Ditton Junction in November 1989, behind 90006. Careful examination of the picture will show that a door has been blown open on the second coach.

A February 1990 rain shower has brightened things up at Crewe, where a southbound express is ready to leave behind Mainline-coloured 90029. The absence of any branding distinguishes this from the full InterCity version.

Class 90s were not common on the East Coast Main Line, but helped out when the class 91s were being overhauled. Passing the site of the sidings at Dringhouses, York, 90024 heads south with an Edinburgh to Kings Cross express in May 1992.

Three locomotives were repainted into European Railway colours, to emphasise intercontinental cooperation. Apart from the mandatory yellow panel, 90129 *Frachtverbindungen* appeared in the DB 'white bib' scheme, and is seen at Headstone Lane working a Felixstowe to Trafford Park Freightliner in September 1992.

Also in September 1992, another Felixstowe to Trafford Park service is double-headed at Headstone Lane, with 90138 and 90130 heading the train. The second loco is in SNCF colours.

In the other direction, a Lawley Street to Felixstowe Freightliner is in the charge of the Belgian-liveried loco. 90128 carries the SNCB colours used on their class 21 and 27 locos, and is named *Vrachtverbinding*. Taken in September 1992.

A close-up view of 90130 *Fretconnection* shows it passing Caledonian Road in October 1992. The colour scheme is that carried by the SNCF Sybic class 26000s, apart from the yellow panel.

An interesting combination of class 90 90139 and class 47 47301 *Centurion* heading an eastbound train of BOC tanks along the freight line at Caledonian Road in February 1993.

A lengthy parcels service, destined for Peterborough, passes the crossing and signal box at Helpston in June 1993. 90019 is named *Penny Black* and carries RES colours. Another photo showing a fully-extended pantograph, needed in conjunction with the road crossing.

Carrying Railfreight Distribution decals, 90141 passes Hatch End in June 1993 with a Dagenham Dock to Halewood freight service, whilst a class 90 heading a down express will shortly overtake it.

Also in RFD colours, 90137 heads away from Stratford and passes Hackney Wick Station with a Freightliner from Felixstowe to Lawley Street in July 1993.

90136 was the locomotive which carried the prototype colours for the European version of Railfreight Distribution. The upper panel on the bodyside is in a dark grey. A full yellow end is carried and, apart from the decals, the words 'Railfreight Distribution' are in red on the lower panel. It is seen at Headstone Lane in August 1993, working a Felixstowe to Trafford Park Freightliner.

90008 *Birmingham Royal Ballet* starts away from Runcorn after its stop with a Liverpool Lime Street to Euston express in September 1993.

An exhibition of the four 'Freight Connection' locos was held at Trafford Park Freightliner Terminal in October 1993. From the left is DB 90129, with SNCB 90128, SNCF 90130 and RFD 90122 *Freight Connection*.

The winter sun illuminates 90005 *Financial Times* leaving Lichfield Trent Valley, following a stop with its Liverpool Lime Street to Euston express in December 1993.

The harvest is in at Colton Junction, where 90017 *Rail Express Systems Quality Assured* heads up the main line with a matched RES Low Fell to King's Cross parcels service in August 1995.

The original Freightliner colour scheme is carried by 90143 *Freightliner Coatbridge*, which is traversing the layout at Stratford with a Tilbury to Crewe Basford Hall service in August 1996.

90129 *Frachtverbindungen* with its Halewood to Dagenham freight service just keeps ahead as 313007 pulls into South Kenton with a Watford Junction to Euston DC lines train. Taken in August 1997.

A GNER Leeds to Kings Cross express rushes past Brookmans Park in July 2002, but with European RFD 90038 as the motive power instead of the more standard class 91.

The DB-liveried class 90 has now been repainted into EWS colours and has been renumbered 90029. Working a Virgin Manchester Piccadilly to Euston express, it is seen at South Kenton in December 2003.

Virgin-liveried 90010 *275 Railway Squadron (Volunteers)* and 90013 *The Law Society* combine to propel a Liverpool Lime Street to Euston express past Headstone Lane in March 2004. This photo clearly shows the difference between the ventilation panels on each body side.

One class 90 received a GNER-style colour scheme, but without any lettering. Seen at Pudding Mill Lane in April 2004, it is working an Anglia Liverpool Street to Norwich express.

Another Norwich-bound express heads past Shenfield in April 2004, being worked by EWS 90029, now renamed *Institute of Civil Engineers*.

The One Franchise, which replaced Anglia, adopted a light grey basic colour, but two locos, 90003 and 90004, carried a dark grey version. The latter is seen at Shenfield on its way to Norwich in June 2004.

A diverted Liverpool Street to Norwich express hurtles through Harlow Town in August 2004, worked by de-virgined 90012 (and any other description would be rude!).

A Crewe to Coatbridge Freightliner approaches Carlisle in August 2005, behind Freightliner 90046. The engine is in what was then the new green colours, but lacks the large owner's word on the body side, and the shadowy backlighting does not bring out the colour.

The pioneer coloured RFD loco, now renumbered 90036, carried a full-size EWS panel. In November 2006, it was seen at Pudding Mill Lane working a Down Norwich express.

For once the clouds don't intrude, and a pair of class 90s show off both Freightliner colour schemes. 90016 and 90045 slog uphill through Cheddington with a Crewe Basford Hall to Felixstowe service in July 2007.

In the standard One livery with small coloured panels, 90009 heads away from Colchester after its stop on the way from Liverpool Street to Norwich, on a misty day in February 2008.

Another colour variation seen on the Great Eastern Norwich expresses was 90021 in the First ScotRail scheme, passing Pudding Mill Lane in April 2008, strangely on the Down slow line.

Another view of First ScotRail 90021, this time entering Colchester with an express from Norwich to Liverpool Street, also in April 2008.

A nice selection of motive power passes Headstone Lane in April 2010, travelling from Norwich to Crewe. The consist comprises National Express 90013 with DRS 47712, 20303 and 37059.

In intermediate National Express ex-One colours, 90013 *The Evening Star: Pride of Ipswich 1885 to 2010 – 125 Years of serving Suffolk*, heads for Norwich after stopping at Colchester in April 2011.

In the new Freightliner Powerhaul scheme, 90045 passes Colchester with a Felixstowe to Crewe Basford Hall intermodal service in April 2011.

Only one class 90 carried the full National Express East Anglia grey and white scheme, 90008 *The East Anglian*. Also seen at Colchester in April 2011, it is working an express from Norwich to London.

The colourful combination of DB Schenker 90036 and First ScotRail 90024 brighten the June 2014 day as they run light engines at Headstone Lane.

Covering non-availability of class 390s on the West Coast Main Line, a loco-hauled coaching set was commissioned – known by enthusiasts as the Pretendolino. With specially-painted DRS 90034 at the head, the Euston to Birmingham service is seen passing Carpenders Park in June 2014.

With Abellio Greater Anglia being the latest franchise holder on the main line to Norwich, etc, their new colour scheme is demonstrated on **90008** *Vice-Admiral Lord Nelson*, seen arriving with an Up service at Colchester in September 2014.

The transport group Malcolm has had two locomotives carrying their designs, one a class 66, the other, seen here, being class 90 90024. It is seen in July 2016 working in conjunction with DB-liveried 90019, passing Scout Green with a Mossend to Daventry Freightliner train.

Class 91

Class 91 91004 arrives at Doncaster in August 1988 with a test train made up with Mark 3 sleeping cars, and with HST power car 43014 acting as a driving trailer, making a powerful combination.

91006 ambles through Welwyn North on double yellows, with a Kings Cross to Leeds service in May 1989. Note the different profile between the loco (suited to Mark 4 stock) and the Mark 3 train set.

91008 makes its way through Huntingdon in May 1988, on its way from Leeds to Kings Cross as a Peterborough-bound class 317 unit enters the Down platform.

A Kings Cross to Leeds express passes Helpston in June 1990 behind 91006 which, like a few others of the class, has had its front skirt temporarily removed (for reasons I know not).

91001 *Swallow* accelerates away from York and passes Dringhouses early one morning in April 1992. It is working an Edinburgh to Kings Cross service. What a nice way to spend an hour here before going to work!

Apart from when the class 91s were maintained at Crewe in their early days, they were always resident on the ECML. However, in June 1993, 91001 *Swallow* and a train set undertook some demonstration runs between Euston and Glasgow Central. A view of this rare event is seen at Hatch End, showing an up service.

A late-afternoon glint, shot near Colton Junction in August 1995, highlights 91013 *Sir Michael Faraday* heading a Kings Cross to Glasgow Central express. This location is another where bushes preclude a similar shot.

91006 has now regained its skirt and is seen passing Retford in July 1996, with a Kings Cross to Leeds train.

March 1997 and GNER has now come on the scene, but all is not well at Kings Cross, where 91001 *Swallow* has had to be removed from its train by Thunderbird 47777 *Restored*. This view gives a good view of the blunt end of the class 91.

In GNER colours with silver letters, 91020 passes Alexandra Palace in October 1997 with a Kings Cross to Glasgow Central express. One GNER coach ruins the otherwise InterCity consist.

A matched GNER consist, with gold letters on 91107 *Newark on Trent*, heads towards Hornsey and Kings Cross as it speeds through Alexandra Palace with an express from Glasgow Central. The low November 2005 sun provides ideal lighting.

Well into the climb to Stevenage, 91109 *The Samaritans* has just passed Hitchin with a Newcastle to Kings Cross express in June 2006.

At Frinkley Crossing, north of Barkston, 91110 *David Livingstone* heads south with a Newcastle to Kings Cross express in August 2006.

Later that same day, a failure of some sort has meant that 91128 *Peterborough Cathedral* has to run blunt end leading with its Kings Cross to Leeds express. Although not unknown, it is uncommon enough to be worth recording.

By February 2008, National Express has now taken over the ECML franchise. On an interim basis, it has modified the GNER colours by removing the orange stripe and letters, and applying a white band, as seen on 91132 passing Brookmans Park with a Newcastle-bound express.

Only one class 91 received the proper National Express colour scheme, 91111, which was passing Ally Pally with an Up Leeds service in July 2008.

In recent times, class 91s have carried a variety of individual colour schemes. One of the most striking was the purple Flying Scotsman scheme carried by 91101, which was caught passing Welwyn Garden City in July 2012, working a Kings Cross to Edinburgh express.

Another one-off also seen at Welwyn GC that day was 91110 *Battle of Britain Memorial Flight*, which was working up from Edinburgh.

One more shot at Welwyn Garden City shows the silver scheme with red stripe, adopted by East Coast Railways, the state-supported operation, which took over when the NX franchise failed. 91113 passes with a Down Leeds service.

91111 commemorated those who gave their lives in the First World War. Named *For The Fallen*, it is caught near Brookmans Park in October 2014, working an Edinburgh service from Kings Cross.

When Virgin took over the ECML franchise, a temporary solution to ownership was the provision of labels on locomotives. With a Red Virgin sticker, 91109 heads past Alexandra Palace with a Down Leeds express in March 2015.

The full Virgin East Coast scheme is carried by 91131, seen leaving Edinburgh Waverley for Kings Cross in March 2016.

91101 *Flying Scotsman* has lost its purple livery, but the Virgin colours are at least embellished with Scottish Saltires on the front end. Approaching Colton Junction in March 2016, it is working a Down Edinburgh express.

An Up Edinburgh express speeds through Doncaster Station in June 2016, with 91110 Battle of Britain Memorial Flight doing the hard work at the rear.

The decorations on 91111 *For The Fallen* varied on each side. Showing the opposite side from that of the earlier photo, the loco is working a York to Kings Cross semi-fast service, which has just passed Colton Junction in July 2016.

Class 92
The open day at Crewe Basford Hall in August 1995 hosted several class 92s. This view of 92040 *Goethe* is of interest since it carries the rare EPS logo, representing the passenger service to be worked by these engines, which never eventuated.

One of the two class 92s to carry Railfreight Distribution decals, 92030 *Ashford,* passes Watford Junction with a Mossend to Hoo Junction freight train in May 2001 (92022 was the other loco).

Super power for an ultra-short Mossend to Wembley service seen at Headstone Lane in January 2005. 92003 *Beethoven* and 92014 *Emile Zola* are in the standard two-tone grey livery, whilst 92031 is in EWS colours.

Standing in the yards at Wembley, 92001 *Victor Hugo* waits for business in May 2006. The shot was taken from a Gatwick Airport to Watford Junction service.

With an EWS label on its side, 92042 *Honegger* heads north past Cathiron in September 2006, working a Daventry to Mossend intermodal service.

In July 2011, 92042, now repainted into DB Schenker red livery, enters Welwyn Garden City with a Dollands Moor to Scunthorpe train of empties. At this point, around 16:00, the loco failed, the length of the train being such as to totally block the lines used by services to and from Moorgate, for over two hours, before being rescued. Commuters were not happy!

Now in good health, 92042 is now seen near Kenton with a lengthy train of Cargo vans from Wembley to Daventry in September 2014.

Another view near Kenton, this time in June 2016, where 92014, now carrying Caledonian Sleeper colours, passes by with three coaches from Wembley, destined for Preston, but actually finishing up at Crewe.